THIS IS ME LETTING YOU GO

HEIDI PRIEBE

AMARYLLIS

AMARYLLIS
An imprint of Manjul Publishing House Pvt. Ltd.
• C-16, Sector 3, Noida, Uttar Pradesh 201301, India
Website: www.manjulindia.com
Registered Office:
• 2nd Floor, Usha Preet Complex,
42, Malviya Nagar, Bhopal 462 003 - India
Distribution Centres
Ahmedabad, Bengaluru, Chennai, Hyderabad,
Kochi, Kolkata, Mumbai, Noida, Pune

This is Me Letting You Go by Heidi Priebe

This edition first published in India in 2024
Second impression 2025

ISBN 978-93-5543-600-9

Cover design © Thought Catalog Books

Printed and bound in India by Thomson Press (India) Ltd.

CONTENTS

For B.

INTRODUCTION

This is a book that I wrote when I was heartbroken.

I'd imagine that's how many books get made.

We lose something we love, and it seems natural to try to reconstruct it—mulling over memories, sorting through missteps, bleeding our expired hopes and habits onto paper, hoping some part of what we've loved will still be salvageable.

If only I can make this pain pretty, we tell ourselves, then it mattered. Then there's some reason to carry it forward.

But real pain isn't pretty at all.

And through the process of writing this book, I learned just that.

This book is a compilation of articles I wrote throughout one of the most tumultuous years of my life.

I was freshly out of college and newly dumped. I was welcoming the job of my dreams and saying goodbye to a community I loved. I was falling in love at some points, and I was falling apart at others. I was ready to move on, and I was wholly unprepared to let go. And isn't that how so many of our changes take place?

Life happens before we are ready for it. These pages are a testament to that.

This is a book about moving on when you don't want to. It's a book about receiving a future you're not ready for. It's a book about accepting that the hand we are dealt is not always the one we want to play, and yet we have to learn to keep on playing anyway.

This is a book about letting go.

It's about letting go of pain and expectation. Of self-loathing and self-glorification. Of the traumas that we never thought we'd heal from and the love that we never thought we'd lose.

This book is a mixture of lighthearted, joyful articles and serious, somber ones. Because the truth about letting go is that it doesn't take on a single shape or form. It happens in stops and starts. In stretches and setbacks. In moments where the world feels wide-open and days where all your doors are slamming shut.

Letting go isn't simple or straightforward. It's a dynamic, lifelong process.

And I hope that some part of this book can meet you wherever you are in that process.

Because nobody else can let go for you. But we could all use some company along the way.

1

READ THIS IF NOBODY TEXTED YOU GOOD MORNING

First of all: Good morning, beautiful.

Is it too late to say that? I know you've probably been awake a while—likely hours or even all day. I know you may have gone this whole time without hearing it—shrugging back to friends and family who asked you how you're doing with a non-committal "Fine" because that is what we're meant to do as humans—answer meaningful questions with arbitrary phrases. I know that you may not be fine. I know you may have had a lackluster day. And I know that something as incredibly mundane as a "Good morning" text may have made all the difference in the world. It's okay if that's the case. It's okay to sometimes ache for those simple and kind-hearted gestures.

Because the truth is that good morning texts are more than a half-hearted means of communication. They are a sign that we are thought of. Cared for. Adored by someone who may not be immediately present. They are a reminder—one we perhaps should not need but sometimes do—that we are appreciated in our entirety. So, if you did not get one this morning, here is what I want you to know:

You deserve to have a good day today, not because of some universal law that necessitates good things happening to worthwhile people, but because we all do. We all deserve to have a beautiful morning and a correspondingly fantastic day, regardless of who loves us, appreciates us, or thinks of us first thing when they wake up in the AM. Just because someone is not around to appreciate the complexities of who you are does not mean you deserve anything less than pure joy. And in case there's no one else to remind you, here is what else I want you to know:

There's a particular way you laugh that can make an entire room light up, if only for a moment in time. There is a way you tilt your head when you are concentrating that makes you look unbearably kissable—as if you were placed on this earth only to stare at things and frown in the most endearing form humanely possible. There is a noise you make when you are falling asleep—a soft, almost inaudible sigh that sounds like the ethereal embodiment of all that is tranquil and calm. There are a thousand minute intricacies that make up the tapestry of who you are, and not a single one has ceased to exist since the last time that somebody loved you.

I know we're not supposed to need reminders of that. I know that we're supposed to be strong and self-sufficient and reassured—certain of our own worth, questioning only the value of others. But we're human. We forget.

We forget that we are lovable. We forget that we're desired. We forget that we are anything other than the hard-shelled, busybody workaholics we've all been trained to behave as. We forget that we, too, merit adoration.

And here's what is easiest to forget: Who you are doesn't cease to exist because there's nobody there to admire it. The way you bite your pencil is still cute, even when nobody teases you for it. How you hold yourself still exudes confidence, even if there's no one to assert it to. The way your eyes light up when you're talking about what you love is—and endlessly will be—attractive, regardless of who is there to listen to you speak. All the little quirks that make you up are not extinguished because somebody once chose against them. You still deserve to have a good day, even when there's no one there to wish it to you. Even if you forget to remind yourself.

Someday, someone's going to love all of those tiny things about you. Someone's going to love the way you cough. They're going to laugh at the way you lose your keys while you're actually holding them. Someday, someone is going to stare at you from across a crowded room and know exactly how you're feeling based on the way your head is tilting or the type of wine you've used to fill your glass. Someone is going to appreciate all of your obscurities eventually, but right now, they are all only your own. And that's okay. First and foremost, you will always belong to yourself.

Here's what I urge of you if you did not receive a good morning text today: Don't forget what makes you incredible. Don't let your own intricacies slide. Because the lovable parts of you are not gone—I absolutely promise you that much.

You are so much more than the person who nobody texted this morning. You are encompassing. You are fierce. You are a blazing, roaring fire in a world full of people who've been burnt. So please, refuse to let the wounded people extinguish you. Refuse to be tamed. Refuse to flicker down into a lump of meager, burnt-out coal because somebody else is not tending to your flame.

At the end of the day, we're all in charge of what we bring to our lives. So be the person who brings light to your own, even if nobody else shows up for it. Be the person who has a good day, even if nobody wishes you to have one. Find a way to fuel your flame when no one else remembers to because the world needs the light you give off.

And you, my dear, are too intense a power to be reduced by something as small and insignificant as the lack of a good morning text.

2

I'M TEXTING YOU THIS BECAUSE I LIKE YOU

I'm texting you this because I like you. Because when I think of you, I get this sort of insane feeling inside of my gut that makes me want to listen to really bad pop songs and go for a run (you know it's bad when I willingly want to go running). I'm texting you this because I think about your body sometimes, pressed up against mine, and what that would mean and how awesome that would feel. I'm texting you this because I like you, and I'm wondering if you've caught on.

I'm texting you this because I want to seem like I don't care. Isn't it insane how we do that as humans—how we have to feign distance and disinterest as a means of expressing how we feel for one another? I think that's just crazy, and I know you do, too. I think that is a good conversation we could have, you and I. The kind we pick up over coffee that ends up dragging on for hours and getting us kicked out of the café when it closes. You know, that's the thing that I like most about you—the way your eyes light up with every new idea and the way the conversation never wanes. I like a lot of things about you, but I'm not going to text those to you because I'm playing it cool. Playing it cool is what we're always meant to do, even though it doesn't really seem to impress you.

I'm not texting you the link to a website because I think you're actually going to like it. I mean, you might, and that would be great, but I mostly just want your reply. What do you think of this thing that I find funny? What in your mind aligns with mine, and where does it deviate? What do I enjoy that you despise? What do you analyze that I glaze over unnoticed? I'm texting you this because I want to know your thoughts on something—anything, really. Your mind is an infinite library that I would like to peruse for a while.

I'm texting you this because I had a bad day. Because my lunch order got messed up, and I didn't say the right thing in that meeting, and my friends bailed on that thing that we were supposed to do tonight. I'm texting you this because when your name flashes across my screen, I temporarily forget about all of the petty annoyances that plague us when we don't think to evade them. Something about you reminds me that there are bigger, better, more important things out there than whether I had almonds in my salad or happy hour is a go.

I'm texting you this because I'm glad I met you. Because before you came along, things were okay, but something about you injected color into my world, and I don't want it to fade out just yet. Because you reminded me that something as simple as human interaction could change a shitty day into a good one and a bland thought into a fascinating argument, and you make me feel like I've had ten hours of sleep and a coffee even when I'm exhausted straight through to the bones. I'm texting you because the rhythm of your mind has gotten stuck inside of mine, and I would like it to stay there for a while.

I'm texting you this because I want to see you again. Because our generation has whittled interaction down into a series of superficial scripts that we exchange with one another on autopilot, but I'm almost okay with the trivialities if they end up leading me to you. Because my phone's charged and my heart's full, and I'm sick of all the tired, useless games we end up playing to disguise our admiration of each other. I am texting you because I want to. Because I want you here beside me, with your thoughts brimming, your breath heavy, and your phone all forgotten and discarded.

I'm texting you this because I like you. And I'm hoping that you like me too.

3

THE TRUTH ABOUT MEETING SOMEONE AT THE WRONG TIME

Timing is something that none of us can seem to get quite right with relationships. We meet the person of our dreams the month before they leave to study abroad. We form an incredibly close friendship with an attractive person who is already taken. One relationship ends because our partner isn't ready to get serious, and another ends because they're getting serious too soon.

"It would be *perfect*," we moan to our friends, "if only this were five years from now/eight years sooner/some indistinct time in the future when all our problems would take care of themselves." Timing seems to be the invariable third party in all of our relationships. And yet, we never stop to consider why we let timing play such a drastic role in our lives.

Timing is a bitch, yes. But it's only a bitch if we let it be. Here's a simple truth that we all need to face up to: *the people we meet at the wrong time are actually just the wrong people.*

You never meet the right people at the wrong time because the right people are timeless. The right people make you want to throw away the plans you originally had for one and follow them into the hazy, unknown future without a glance backward. The right people don't make you hem and haw about whether or not you want to be with them; you just know. You know that any adventure you had originally planned out for your future isn't going to be half as incredible as the adventures you could have by their side. That no matter what you thought you wanted before, this is better. Everything has been better since they came along.

When you are with the right person, time falls away. You don't worry about fitting them into your complicated schedule because they become a part of that schedule. They become the backbone of it. Your happiness becomes your priority, and so long as they are contributing to it, you can work around the rest.

The right people don't stand in the way of the things you once wanted and make you choose them over those things. The right people encourage you to try harder, dream bigger, and do better. They bring out the most incredible parts of yourself and make you want to fight harder than ever before. The right people don't impose limits on your time, your dreams, or your abilities. They want to tackle those mountains with you, and they don't care how long it takes. With the right person, you have all the time in the world.

The truth is, when we pass someone up because the timing is wrong, what we are really saying is that we don't care to spend our time on that person. There will never be a magical time when everything falls into place and fixes all our broken relationships. But there may someday be a person who makes the issue of timing irrelevant.

Because when someone is right for us, we make the time to let them into our lives. And that kind of timing is *always* right.

4

READ THIS IF YOU'RE WORRIED THAT YOU'LL NEVER FIND 'THE ONE'

Imagine something crazy for me quickly.

What if you peered into a fortune ball right now—this very second, today—and saw with indisputable clarity that you were never going to meet the love of your life?

That's a sad thing I'm asking you to think of, I'm aware. You've been hoping to meet "The One" for a while now—or at least someone half-decent who you can deal with for the rest of your life. I know, I know. You're not fanciful like everyone else. You don't believe in soulmates. But you were expecting to meet someone you liked a fair amount. Someone to curl up next to at the end of a long day, who would take care of you when you got sick and listen to your stories every evening after work. We all hope that. We're human.

But imagine for a second that you knew—with 100% certainty—that you would never meet that person. What about your life would that knowledge change?

Because here's the thing about finding love—it affects us constantly. And we all loathe admitting it. But love is at the forefront of our actions even when it's not at the forefront of our minds. It's the reason you bought those new jeans last week. It's the reason you went to that barbecue that you didn't want to go to last weekend. It's the reason you sometimes feel cripplingly insecure and inadequate and scared about everything that's coming next. Love's what inspires most of your greatest changes.

So, if you knew, with indisputable certainty, that love was never going to be yours, how would you live your life differently? What about your daily routine would you alter? What about your long-term plans?

Your first inclination may be to say "Nothing." After all, you're a smart person. You have plans that don't involve someone else's influence. We all do. But ponder it a few moments more. Because here's what we don't want to admit about love: it is a crutch we use all the time. The idea that someday somebody will love all our flaws is a subtle excuse not to work on them. The principle of two halves making a whole restrains us from becoming our own better half. We want someone to swoop in during our darkest hour and save us, but what if we knew they never would? We'd have to start doing everything differently.

If you knew that love would never be an option for you, what would be? How would you structure the rest of your life? Would it focus more on career—a stronger inclination toward success? Or would you use the time to invest in yourself—go on a few more vacations, travel further outside your comfort zone? If you knew that you would never again feel the rush of budding romance, where would you turn to for your thrills? How would you get your blood pumping?

And what about your other relationships—would they suddenly take on more weight? Would you spend more time appreciating your family, if you knew that they are the people who will have loved you the most strongly at the end of your life? What about your friendships? Would you nurture and care more for the people who love you platonically if you knew nobody would ever love you romantically? Would you show up a little more often or share a little more of your life?

My inclination is to believe that never finding love would be a game-changer for most of us. One we'd initially consider devastating but may eventually realize is the ultimate liberation. Without the fear of ending up alone, the opportunities open to you would become endless. You could live on every continent. You could scale the corporate ladder. You could go back to school and get that degree you've always felt interested in without worrying about the financial burden your debt may place on somebody else. Love holds us back in an infinite amount of subtle ways that perhaps we do not even realize. And the guarantee of its absence may just be the ultimate sense of liberation.

Because if we didn't have to search for the love of our lives, we would finally be free to realize that we are allowed to be the loves of our own. That we can spend our lives developing ourselves, challenging ourselves, pampering ourselves, and building ourselves up to be bigger, more capable people than we ever once hoped to become. We could become everything we've been searching for. We could construct our soulmates in ourselves.

If there's one thing we all need to stop doing, it's waiting around for someone else to show up and change our lives. Just be the person you've been waiting for. Live your life as if you are the love of it. Because that's the only thing you know for sure—that through every triumph, every failure, every fear, and every gain that you will ever experience until the day you die, you are going to be present. You are going to be the person who shows up to accept your rewards. You are going to be the person who holds your own hand when you're broken. You are going to be the person who gets yourself up off the floor every time you get knocked down, and if those things are not love-of-your-life qualities, I don't know what are.

We have to start appreciating all that we bring to our own lives. Because the ironic truth is, you are most attractive when you're not worried about who you're attracting. When you're living your life confidently, freely, and without restraint, you emit the kind of energy that isn't possible to fake. The kind of energy capable of transforming not just your own life but the lives of people around you.

So stop looking for The One to spend the rest of your life with. Be The One.

And let everybody else come searching for you.

5

FOR EVERY FIERCE WOMAN WHO HAS TRIED TO BE TAME

I know you.

I know that you have always felt different—a little bit more restless than perhaps you ought to be as a child. A little less timid, a tad bit too brash. I know you've grown up with inklings of suspicion—that your mind does not work the way it should, perhaps. Your thoughts whirl around at strange speeds, and you cannot seem to reel yourself in.

I know that you have tried to settle down—tried to calm your passions, cool your fire, and slip into the steady existence that seems to lull everyone else into oblivion. I know you have reasoned with your instincts, rationalized your desires, and fought against the churning chaos inside your bloodstream that tells you to always seek more. To always do more. To always be more than was ever expected of you.

I know the visions of love that you were taught as a child do not appeal to you—you do not want the dependency, the complacency, the fairy-tale story that everyone else seems to want. I know you're dying for someone to tell you that this does not mean you're incapable of love. That you simply have not found the right person yet—the one who wakes up in the night burning with the same fire that burns inside you, thrumming with the same energy that drives you and reeling on forward with the same sort of reckless abandon that beckons you, too. I know you long to be told that you do not have to tone yourself down to a smaller, frailer, more helpless version of yourself in order to be loved. You just have to wait a little longer, run a little further, and come across that great love a little bit differently. You are the flame, not the moth. And your job is to burn with conviction.

I know it hasn't always been easy. I know that life has been a constant tug-of-war for you, no matter where you go. You have stayed when you wanted to leave. Held on when you wanted to give in. Been at ends with your own exhausted mind about what makes you happy because you do not want the things you were once taught to desire. And that's okay. It is okay in a way that you have never been told, perhaps because you've never met anyone like you. And that is a shame. It is a shame there aren't more people like you.

I know you're not as wild as they think you are. I know you've been torn more than once. I know you've felt the pull of both coming and going, of loving and leaving, of settling down and breaking free. I know you seek the tiny comforts that others don't expect from you—having someone to report to when you're far away, having somewhere to come home to when your adventuring is done. I know you are a series of infinite contradictions within yourself, and you would like to understand them so badly that some days you want to scream. You want to rip the inconsistencies out of your body and learn to live simply and whole-heartedly. I know that for you, whole-hearted will always be a transient state. Happiness will always be an ever-moving target. Fulfillment will never be a subway stop that you get off at. It will forever be the chase, the fervor, the constant need for more.

I know you despise these clichés. I know you do not want a heart that is both wild and tame in its most shameless state. I know you would give it all up in an instant to be one way or another, to not remain split between the storm and the silence within you. I know you get tired of yourself. And I'm sorry—that you've ever felt exhausted by the person that you are.

For the fierce women who've tried to be tame, I applaud you. For how you live your lives and for the times you don't apologize. For the fierceness of your spirit and the strength inside your soul. I applaud you for undergoing life with that fearless and bold-hearted attitude—the one that speaks the mind of so many others like you. The world needs more women like you. The world needs to revel and behold you.

For every fierce woman who's tried to be tame, I hope you know—there's a place in this world for wild hearts like yours. And the sooner you stop trying to fight it, the sooner you're already home.

6

YOU SHOULD CHOOSE THE LIFESTYLE YOU WANT OVER THE PERSON YOU WANT

Life presents us with a lot of hard choices.

What clothing to put on in the morning. Milk or cream in our coffee. Who to spend the rest of our lives with, and what to do if we want completely different things out of it than they do.

There are pre-designed answers to these questions, of course. High-waisted jeans. Milk is less fattening. Pick the person you want to be with because love conquers all. We have a specific set of rules we ought to follow as we plow through the tough questions in our lives, and they all come with pre-determined outcomes.

The outcome of choosing the right pants is getting complimented by the trendy girl in your office. Picking milk means you won't feel as bloated. Picking the person you love over the life that you want means your sense of self-worth will slowly degrade and deteriorate over years of contentedly slipping into bed beside someone you're comfortable with.

I want to make it clear that I'm not bashing marriage. Or relationships. Or romance of any kind. I love love. I love it too much. I lose my mind, heart, and footing over love much more often than I'd like to admit, and that's the only reason I know anything about this in the first place. Love is wonderful, worthwhile, and enriching, but it should never be a standoff between the person and the life you want.

Love shouldn't have to be the biggest compromise of your life. I know that you've been told otherwise. You've watched movies, read novels, and heard adages from relatives and friends who perhaps have very successful relationships—love requires constant compromise. You can't have it all. And perhaps they are right. You can't have it all. But you should be able to have what matters.

You should be able to be with somebody you love and also live a life that entices, invigorates, and inspires you. You should be able to pursue what you want out of this world in every fearless way you want to without running the risk of losing the person you value most. You should be able to have, at the bare minimum, a relationship that allows for growth and exploration on the part of both parties.

What you have when you have a relationship that forces you to whittle or water yourself down is a mismatch of values. You may have found someone you love. Even someone you want to spend your life with. But if the only time you see eye-to-eye is when you're staring into each other's, you're signing yourself up for a lifetime of hard choices.

You can make it work with someone who wants different things than you. It's been done countless times. If one wants a steady 9-5 and the other wants to endlessly roam the globe, you can find an in-between. One can settle down, or the other can speed up, or you can find a satiated in-between where both of you are halfway to happy. But is this the life either of you really want? Is this the life you'll be happy with when you look back at it? Will you be glad you compromised and put aside your desires for another person?

If the answer is yes, then you're set. Some compromises are worth it. But if the answer is no, I encourage you to move on. To cut the cord. To do the hard thing that none of us want to do and to go pursue the life that you wish you were living.

Here's the stark truth about the person who is right for you: They want the same lifestyle that you do. How do I know this? Because that is, by definition, what makes them right for you. To be with someone whose eyes light up when yours do, whose heart races when your blood also pounds, who is enticed and inspired by the same forces that drive you forward, is a gift many of us never truly get to experience.

Because we settle. We settle for the person we love over the person who could push us—to be bigger, stronger, greater versions of ourselves. We tell ourselves that love is enough. That it conquers everything. But we forget that love shouldn't be the thing that conquers our lives—we should be. And we should do it deliberately, triumphantly, by the side of somebody who shares all of our joys and successes.

So how do we meet such a person? That's simple—we do more of what we love. We give ourselves up to uncertainty, to searching, to pursuing what we want out of life without the certainty of having someone beside us while we do it. We throw ourselves wholeheartedly into the things that we love, and we consequently attract the people who love what we love. Who value what we prioritize. Who appreciate all that we are. We throw ourselves into the heart of possibility instead of staying comfortably settled inside of certainty. Because we owe it to ourselves to do so. We owe it to ourselves to live the greatest life that we're capable of living, even if that means that we have to be alone for a very long time.

At the end of the day, love is wonderful, but it isn't enough to make up for an entire lifetime of compromising your core values. You don't want to spend forever gazing into somebody's eyes, expecting to find all of the answers you need inside of them. Wait for the person who is gazing outward in the same direction as you are.

It's going to make all of the difference in the world.

7

HOW TO FALL HALF IN LOVE WITH SOMEONE

To fall half in love with someone, be alone.

Be alone for so long that you forget how to properly fall, that you forget anything but sideways glances and chance encounters and whomever you're standing closest to when the bar lights come on at the end of the night.

To fall half in love, lose faith in people. Decide that everyone leaves and everyone screws up and that you are more than included in that pool. Tell yourself that there was a time and a place for love, but it was long, long ago, and not here. Decide that for a long time, half-hearted replications are all that you're going to get. Decide that nothing's going to feel like it once did, and let that be okay. Let yourself accept that as a cold, inevitable truth.

To fall half in love, make a mistake. Linger one moment too long at a bar or café. Invite the wrong person into your bed. Listen too intently to somebody's story and fail to realize that we can fall in love entirely accidentally. Fail to realize the moment in which the chain-link barrier around your heart lowers and lets something in because it has been up for so long that you forgot it was not entirely indestructible. For a long time, fail to realize that you can feel anything at all.

To fall half in love with someone, recognize it too late. Realize in an offhanded moment that the lilt of their laugh makes you breathless, that the taste of their lips drives you mad. Find yourself transfixed with the movement of their hands as they're brewing a simple cup of coffee and realize that something has shifted deep inside of you, something it's too late to put back.

To fall half in love with someone, jump ship. Realize that you're not ready for full love, for real love, for the kind of love that nurtures and catches and heals. Realize that you've been alone for so damn long because you have a world of your own making, and you like it there. That the touch of someone's hand shouldn't make you weak, that the sound of their voice shouldn't haunt you. To fall half in love, leave before you have the chance to fall fully because you aren't ready to let that overtake you. You aren't prepared to wander through that wasteland again.

To fall half in love with someone, move on. Go confidently forward in the direction of whatever life you'd had planned long before they ever came along.

But every now and then, let your mind wander back.

Every now and then, remain transfixed on the memory of their skin against yours, of their hands in your hair, of the quiet, patient moments where laughter unexpectedly escaped your lips lying beside them. Let your mind wander back until you realize that it's not them you're missing at all—it's the unfulfilled possibility they embodied.

Because the truth is, you never really did fall in love with them.

You fell in love with their potential. You fell in love with the maybes and the could-have-beens. You fell in love with all the trips you didn't take, the plans you didn't make, the hazy, unintelligible future that stretched out before you without any opportunity to build upon. You fell in love with the potential of what could have happened had you been the kind of person who'd stayed. Had you been the person who could fall in love fully, without pause.

You realize that you didn't fall in love with them at all but that you could have. That you might have. That there may always be a small part of yourself that is going to wonder '*what if*,' and that maybe you like it that way.

That maybe you prefer only falling half in love because it allows you to write your own ending to the story.

And theirs is a story that you want to still have and hold onto years down the line when you need something to write on and on and on.

8

READ THIS WHEN YOU'RE TIRED OF EVERYTHING

I know what it's like to feel tired—and not just in the physical sense.

The world that we live in is an exhausting place to be. It is wearing. It is thankless. It is endlessly trying and scarcely rewarding. You're tired simply because you live in it. You're tired of loving too much, caring too much, giving too much to a world that never gives anything back. You are tired of investing in indefinite outcomes. You're tired of uncertainties. Tired of grey.

I know you haven't always been this worn out—that there was a time when you were hopeful and pure. When your optimism outweighed your cynicism, and you had an infinite amount in you to give. I know you have been chipped away and worn down piece by piece—a broken heart here and an unkept promise there. I know the world hasn't always been kind throughout the games you've played and that you've lost more times than you have ever won. I know you're feeling uninspired to try again. I know.

Because the truth is, we're all tired. Every single one of us. By a certain age, we are all nothing more than an army of broken hearts and aching souls desperately searching for fulfillment. We want more, but we're too tired to ask for it. We're sick of where we are, but we are too scared to begin again. We need to take risks, but we're afraid to watch it all come crashing down around us. After all, we're not sure how many times we will be able to start over.

We all think we're alone in our exhaustion. But the truth is we're tired of each other—tired of the games we play, the lies we tell, and the uncertainties we present to each other. We don't want to play the villain, but we don't want to play the fool, either. So our guards go up. Our defenses rile. And we take on the role that we loathe to see played because we're not sure what choice we have left.

I know how impossible it can feel to go on trying and giving and becoming when you are exhausted straight through to the soul. I know that the cheerful ideals you were once promised now seem tired and hopeless. But here's what I beg if you're this close to giving up: give it one more try with feeling. I know you're tired of your attempts. I know that you're at your wit's end. But the truth about that second wind of passion is that you're never going to realize you have it if you do not keep on running past your first.

We're all more resilient than we think, and that's an indisputable truth. There is always more love that we are capable of giving, more hope that we are capable of having, more passion that we're capable of unleashing and flooding out into the world. We just don't walk far enough down our own roads to reach the point where we're seeing those actions pay off. We want immediate results, and when we see none, we give up. We let the exhaustion stop us. We grow frustrated with the lack of feedback, and we assume that means we have to throw the entire attempt right out the window.

Because here's something we all loathe to admit—none of us feel inspired every day. We all get exhausted. We all get discouraged. And we're allowed to work on through those feelings. Just because you're beaten down and worn out and sick of the life that you're living doesn't mean you're not making a change. Every person you have ever admired has had times when they felt utterly defeated in the pursuit of their dreams. But that didn't prevent them from reaching them. You're allowed to stumble slowly towards your biggest transformations. It doesn't always have to be a blazing, flagrant affair.

Some parts of life happen quietly. They happen slowly. They happen because of the small, careful choices that we make every day that turn us into better versions of ourselves. We have to allow ourselves the time to let those alterations happen. To watch them evolve. To avoid growing hopelessly frustrated in the in-between.

When you're tired, go slowly. Go quietly. Go timidly. But do not stop. You are tired for all the right reasons. You are tired because you're supposed to be. You're tired because you're making a change. You are exhausted for all the right reasons, and it's only an indication to go on. You are tired because you're growing. And someday, that growth will give way to the exact rejuvenation you need.

9

HERE IS HOW YOU LOVE WITHOUT EXPECTATION

Here is how you love without expectation:

You love yourself first. Not necessarily most or best, but first. You don't cancel plans that you were excited about because somebody else wanted your time. You don't rearrange your schedule to accommodate someone who may bail at the last moment anyway. You are strict with yourself—even when you want to give in to the impulses of others—because you know that what you want and what you need is not always the same thing.

You need someone you can rely on, and that person has to be you. At the end of the day, if everyone else bails and flakes and fails to show, you will still be there. So don't look at yourself as a sad consolation prize. Put in the work. Become someone you're proud of. If you're who you're left with at the end of the day, be happy with who you've ended up with. Make sure it's someone you'd pick over a flakey, unreliable love interest or friend.

To love without expectation, you choose honesty in your own endeavors. If you don't want games, you stop playing them. You text back. You show up. You say what you mean, and you don't make time for maybes. In a world full of dishonest people, you choose not to become one of them, even if that makes you lose a foolish game or two. Like attracts like, and if you're looking for straightforward, no-nonsense people, you will have to become one. So you wean out a few losers on the way there. So what. You're becoming who you want to be.

To love without expectation, you show compassion. You remember the times when you've lied and cheated and fell short of the expectations other people set for you, and you forgive yourself for them. You understand that you had a liability, but you did not live up to it, and while you may not be okay with your choices, there was a reason why the cards fell the way they did. You remember that reason. You remember that other people may have similar reasons when they let you down—reasons that have nothing to do with you at all.

You learn to detach from your personal investment in why people do what they do because chances are, it doesn't exist. You understand that you have infinitely less to do with other people's actions than you've always believed. And you learn to be fine with that. Learn to be free within it, even.

To love without expectation, you learn what's not in your control. You understand that everyone has their own demons to contend with, and nobody owes it to anyone else to fight them. At the end of the day, you have two choices in love—one is to accept someone just as they are, and the other is to walk away. There is no in-between. There is no bartering, bargaining, expecting, and falling short in love. There is just choosing to be there or not. Anything in between is a tired, self-interested excuse for love.

To love without expectation, you learn to appreciate what's there. Other people are not ours to own or rearrange or expect things from, and the more anticipation we put onto others, the more we let ourselves down in the end. All we can do is appreciate who we have when we have them and let them go when we do not. To lend our hearts like vacant hotel rooms: celebrating others when they come in and letting them go when they leave. Understanding that at the end of the day, all we can do is refuse occupancy. But we cannot force anyone to stay.

To love without expectation, you have to be okay with yourself. Okay with opening your doors, spreading your arms, baring your heart, and understanding that not everyone will be gentle with it. You have to know that you can recover from those aches, that you can heal your own wounds, and that you can trust yourself to walk away from the situations that do not grow or aid you.

Because here's the thing about placing expectations on others: at the root of expectation is need. Need for others to accept you, to validate you, to tell you that you're good and worthwhile and strong. And if you can do that for yourself—if you can live up to your own expectations and desires, then the need for other people to do so disappears. The need to bend over backward, accommodate others, and seek validation from those who do not deserve your heart disappears.

Who to love and who to leave becomes simple. And expectation slides out the window.

10

READ THIS IF THERE'S SOMEONE YOU CAN'T FORGIVE

I hate every cliché that exists about forgiveness.

I know every adage, every piece of advice, every regularly endorsed opinion on the topic because I've scoured my way through the literature. I've read every blog post about letting go of anger. I've written down Buddha quotes on Post-its and stuck them to my wall. I know that no part of it is simple. I know the adages are tired. I know the gap between "deciding to forgive" and actually feeling peace can seem entirely unbridgeable. I know.

Forgiveness is a vast, un-traversable land for those who crave justice. The very thought of letting someone walk away scot-free from what they've done makes us sick. We don't want to simply wipe our hands clean. We want to transfer the blood onto theirs. We want to see the scores evened and the playing field leveled. We want them to bear the weight of their actions, not us.

Forgiveness seems like the ultimate betrayal of yourself. You don't want to give up the fight for justice after what has happened to you. The anger is burning inside you and pumping toxicity throughout your system. You know that, but you can't let it go. The anger is as inseparable a part of you as your heart, mind, or lungs. I know the feeling. I know the second heartbeat that is fury.

But here's the thing about anger: it's an instrumental emotion. We stay angry because we want justice. Because we think it's useful. Because we assume that the angrier we are, the more change we will be capable of incurring. Anger doesn't realize that the past is over and the damage has been done. It tells you that vengeance will fix things. It's on the pursuit of justice.

Except the justice we want isn't always realistic. Staying angry is like continually picking the scab off a cut because you think that if you keep the wound open, you won't get a scar. It's thinking that someday, the person who wronged you can come give you stitches with such incredible precision that you'll never know the cut was once there. The truth about anger is that it's nothing more than the refusal to heal because you're scared to. Because you're afraid of who you'll be once your wounds close up and you have to go on living in your new, unfamiliar skin. You want your old skin back. And so anger tells you to keep that wound bleeding.

When you're seething, forgiveness seems impossible. We want to be capable of it because, intellectually, we know it's the healthiest choice to make. We want the peace forgiveness offers. We want the release. We want the madness in our brains to quiet down, yet we cannot find a way to get there.

Because here's what they all fail to tell you about forgiveness: It's not going to fix anything. It's not an eraser that will wipe away the pain of what's happened to you. It does not undo the pain that you've been living with and grant you immediate peace. Finding peace is a long, uphill battle. Forgiveness is just what you take to stay hydrated along the way.

Forgiveness means giving up hope for a different past. It means knowing that the past is over, the dust has settled, and the destruction left in its wake can never be reconstructed to resemble what it was. It's accepting that there's no magic solution to fix the damage. It's the realization that as unfair as the hurricane was, you still have to live in its city of ruins.

And no amount of anger is going to reconstruct that city. You have to do it yourself.

Forgiveness means accepting responsibility—not for causing the destruction, but for cleaning it up. It's the decision that restoring your own peace is finally a bigger priority than disrupting someone else's.

Forgiveness doesn't mean you must make amends with those who hurt you. It doesn't mean befriending them, sympathizing with them, or validating what they have done to you. It just means accepting that they've left a mark on you. And that, for better or for worse, that mark is now your burden to bear. It means you're done waiting for the person who broke you to come put you back together. It's the decision to heal your wounds, regardless of which marks they will leave on your skin. It's the decision to move forward with scars.

Forgiveness isn't about letting injustice reign. It's about creating your own justice, your own karma, and your own destiny. It's about getting back onto your feet and deciding that the rest of your life isn't going to be miserable because of what happened to you. It means walking bravely into the future with every scar and callous you've incurred along the way. Forgiveness means saying that you're not going to let what happened to you define you any longer.

Forgiveness doesn't mean that you are giving up all of your power. Forgiveness means you're finally ready to take it back.

11

THE WORST KIND OF FAILURE THAT NOBODY TALKS ABOUT

Whether you've noticed it or not, we talk a lot about failure.

There are endless inspirational articles about it. They tell you about falling down and getting back up. About resilience and endurance. About the thousands of successful people who first failed and how we, too, can be heroic and successful just like them. I know that these articles exist because I've written a few of them myself. And I believe them with all my heart—failure can be a noble and empowering experience. Except for when it's not.

Because here's the harsh truth about failure: It's not always going to be pretty. It's not always going to be endearing. Failure isn't always going to be a product of external circumstances wreaking havoc. Sometimes, it will be entirely a product of our own unmoderated judgment. The situations we manipulated carelessly. The hearts we were clumsy and rough with. The things that we risked and then lost. The failures that are hardest to recover from are the ones that we walked into willingly and selfishly, thinking they'd lead us somewhere better. They are the failures that kick us off our own team.

Every inspirational article on failure talks about believing in yourself and bouncing back. But we don't talk about what it feels like to not want to believe in ourselves anymore in the wake of a mistake. We don't talk about what it feels like when it seems we don't deserve to get up off the floor and try again. We don't talk about the shame accompanying those huge, avoidable errors we make because we eternally want that silver lining that saves us from ourselves. And we can't bear the thought that there may not be one.

Not all failures are worthy of redemption—and that's the cold, hard truth. You may never see the silver lining. Years from now, you may look back on what you've done and, as humans tend to do, assign some sort of arbitrary meaning to it—some sense of "I would not have gotten here without having been there," but it may never be enough to dissolve the lump inside of your throat. It may never fill up the whole that failure carved out inside of you.

And so often, this has to do with the process that brought you to failure. We fail with elegance when we are proud of who we are. When we can stand behind the choices we made. But if we can't, our errors swallow us whole. When you're knocked from a villainous pedestal, that sense of failure is crippling because it leaves you alone with yourself. It forces you to face up to every wrong decision that led you up to that point and to realize who you've become as a result. I understand that more than anyone. I've been somebody whom I am not proud of, too.

Failure isn't always about learning a lesson, and to imply as much is demeaning to everyone involved. Some mistakes invoke too much collateral damage to merit a positive spin. So, let's simply call failures the one thing they always are—change. Because, by definition, our failures alter everything.

We won't always get a glorious comeback from our mistakes—and so we shouldn't. Some failures aren't about bouncing right back up and giving it another go. Some failures are about genuine change. Intensive self-reflection. And coming to the deep understanding that you can't go on living the way you have been.

Some catastrophes are not there to teach you a lesson but to stop you in your tracks. To humble you. To disassemble the parts of yourself that were operating from a place of pain and to destroy them before they take you over. Some failures are as painful and as disarming as they are because they're there to hold you back from an even worse fate—a life that brings you further and further away from the person you want to be. Some failures are not a lesson learned but a lesson forced. And it's so often the exact lesson we need.

So here's what we do when we get knocked off that pedestal: We get up. Not because we're empowered. Not because we necessarily deserve to. Not because we ought to give whatever twisted goal we were pursuing another go but because we owe it to the world to get up. To make a change. To let our failures resonate and alter us in ways we would never have previously considered.

We cannot spend our time hoping that our big failures will make sense later on. We have to make them make sense. We have to choose our own ending. We have to change as a deliberate and direct result of whatever we have failed at. Let that change be your apology to yourself or the Universe or anyone who got caught up as collateral damage along the way. Let the rest of your life be the apology that you, your loved ones, and the Universe needs from you. Let that be you getting back up.

We don't talk about our huge, overwhelming, most shameful failures because we don't want to admit what they reveal about who we are. But therein lies the choice—you get to decide, after every failure, every defeat, every life-altering mistake—what kind of person you are. What kind of person you've been. And what kind of person you're finally ready to become instead.

12

14 THINGS IT'S TIME YOU FORGAVE YOURSELF FOR

1. The big things that you changed your mind about.
The dream job you never thought you'd quit. The person you didn't think you'd leave. The plans you had for the future that never came to fruition because something else got in the way. Life ebbs and flows, and to keep up with it, we must do the same. We have to forgive ourselves for having the self-awareness to change our minds about the really big things.

2. The ways in which you fought through pain.
The dark paths you shouldn't have gone down. The crazy things you did in the name of coping that brought about more damage than good. The things you did to keep yourself alive when you didn't know any better way. The way your survival instinct showed itself when you were too young or helpless to control it doesn't make you a bad person. It makes you a stronger, fuller person for still being around. For having found your way back to life.

3. The person you could never love properly.
The person whose words and body never fit right with yours, whose thoughts weren't the yin to your yang, whose words never quite sounded right but whom you tried to love despite and because of it all. The person you tried to get it right with so hard that it felt like your heart would give up on beating, but who eventually had to let go. You cannot force

love into existence. And letting it bloom somewhere else only makes us all freer in the end.

4. The fries that you ate with your lunch.
You'll survive this.

5. All the ways in which you are not enough.
The body you'll never have, the knowledge you will never acquire, the courage you'll never muster, and the effort you'll never put in. You may never be brave enough or smart enough or strong enough to suit someone else's ideal, but you are always going to be just perfectly *you* enough, and the moment you realize how important that is, the sooner you can let the rest go.

6. The way you treated your parents when you were sixteen. (Or twenty. Or thirty.)
You were awful and infuriating and insufferable, and now all of those days are behind you (Unless they're not. If you are sixteen and reading this, please hug your parents and tell them you love them). So perhaps we all grew a little sideways or backward on the way to growing up, and we said a couple of things we didn't mean. Life went on. We all grew from it. And it is never too late to say, "I'm sorry."

7. The way you treated yourself most of your life.
Every flaw you picked apart inside the mirror. Every lie you told yourself about your limitations. Every "I am not good enough" thought that ever flitted through the recesses of your mind, settling into a place where it mattered. We have to forgive ourselves for not being our own best friends, our own confidants, and our own biggest cheerleaders. We didn't know what a difference it would make to love ourselves until we finally did.

8. The useless degree you took in college.
The world is changing quickly. Once upon a time, there really were jobs for undergraduate Philosophy majors. We just don't happen to live in that world anymore. But the cool thing about the world we do live in is that it's getting smaller every day. We have less specific career paths when

we graduate but more general opportunities. You'd be shocked by all the ways your "useless" major still comes in handy. You won't end up where you expected, but may end up somewhere much better.

9. The breaks that you took from life.

The semester when life got you down. The year you spent living at home. The months of self-loathing and fear that you wish you could wipe from your mind. We all get overwhelmed sometimes. We all forget how to deal. We need these times to re-group, to reflect, to re-create ourselves, and to figure out where to go next. We are stronger for having gone through these breaks, despite what they felt like at the time. We figured out how to bounce back harder.

10. The chances you didn't take.

The places you never traveled to. The experiences you didn't have. The person you did not chase after when they decided to walk away. We have to unclasp our palms and let go of every alternate reality where we're happier, stronger, and brighter because of all the things we did differently. Those universes do not exist. But ours does. And it's okay here if we open our eyes and let it be.

11. The things you didn't say until it was too late.

The "I love yous" we let slide. The phone calls we didn't pick up. The messages we forgot to pass on while we still had the chance to do so. We believe our words and intentions could have changed things, so we use our words now. We don't let our "I love yous" slide. We pick the phone up. And we forgive ourselves for all the times when we didn't.

12. The disasters you didn't see coming.

Every person you should not have trusted. Every fun night out that went wrong. Every choice that, in retrospect, should not have been made. Except we don't live our lives in retrospect. We live them forward. And we don't get the privilege of knowing if our choices will be right or wrong before we make them. We simply have to do the best we can, try the best we can, and forgive ourselves whenever we are wrong. If we're living life right, we're going to be wrong a whole lot.

13. Whatever you still are not ready for.
Every fear that is holding you back right now. Every leap of faith you haven't yet made. Every story you're telling yourself about where you ought to be by the age that you're currently at. We're all a little not ready for life. We're all a little bit timid. We're all a little bit gun-shy, and we're all trying in whatever small ways we know how. Give yourself the time you need to grow. It's going to happen, just not on the timeline you think it will.

14. The mistakes you haven't even made yet.
Because as much as we'd always like to believe that we're eternally out of the woods now, we're not. We're going to screw up again. We're going to fall down again. We're going to make other huge, inconsolable mistakes that will diminish us. And thank God. The day we stop making mistakes is the day we stop living. We just have to give ourselves the room we need to make them.

13

HERE IS WHEN YOU NEED TO BE ALONE

You need to be alone when you are not at home with yourself. When spending a night by yourself makes you want to tremble and take cover from the storm that rages on inside your mind, you need to learn to find your own shelter. When you want someone else to come and hold you close just to distract you from yourself, you need to learn to hold your own hand. We can love one another, but nobody can save us from ourselves, and when we don't understand that in the slightest, we need to be alone the most.

You need to be alone when you're unhappy with yourself. When your flaws and shortcomings are things you hope someone will someday love away, rather than inadequacies that you resolve to work on within yourself. When you're hoping that someone is going to come along and save you from the mess that you've created, you need to learn to put yourself back together. You need to learn what you have to offer, not just what you can take. You have to learn to be the person who saves you.

You need to be alone when you can't look at another human being—not from across the subway or the table or the sheets that are bunched up between you—and not imagine what it's going to feel like once it's over. When every new beginning is just another reminder of each painful ending that preceded it, you are not ready to start over. The person you're going to fall in love with deserves all your beginnings and none of your endings. If you're still torn up about the past, and it is bleeding straight into the future, it might mean that you need more time to heal. You need to be alone when you cannot arrive anywhere with your whole heart because love requires every last piece of it.

You need to be alone when you want to be selfish. You cannot sacrifice and compromise yourself into a different version of yourself—one who wants less and accommodates more and is happy to make the sort of sacrifices that you abhor. You are who you are, and if you cannot for the life of you focus on another human being because you're thinking of the class or the job fair or the event you'd rather be at when you are lying in bed beside them, then you need to go out and do whatever it is that you would rather be doing. You're more selfish for stringing along someone who thinks you are willing to make sacrifices for them than you would be for calling a spade a spade and living your life unapologetically.

You need to be alone when things are changing. When your old world starts to suffocate, and your new one begins to expand, it is so easy to grab the closest hand you see and holler, "Look! Look at the world expanding!" Because everything is chaotic and wonderful and new, except it's hard to frolic forward with your hand clasped inside somebody else's. At some point, you will want to break away into a run. And if you're someone who needs to run alone, that's okay. It's good to want to explore the options available to you in as unconstrained a fashion as possible. It is okay to need to do that on your own.

You need to be alone when you are growing into a new version of yourself. When you are shedding the layers of who you've been like snakeskin, you will need the time to bury who you've been. We emerge into our new selves so carelessly—tripping over the edges and unfastened parts of who we have not quite figured out how to be. We need time to adjust to the shoes that we're only slowly starting to step into. We need time to figure out who we will become.

You need to be alone when you're not ready. When you meet someone patient and kind and well-meaning, and yet some part of you is holding back. You must know that it is no one else's job to break down the walls you've built up—that is a fortress of your own responsibility. When you are not ready to give someone your whole heart out of fear of what they'll do with it, it is yourself that you must learn how to trust. It's yourself you must come back to, piece by careful piece, as you learn that your heart is an endless, refillable vessel that does not deplete and fall apart when it is given away. It is yourself that you must learn to be alone with.

You need to be alone whenever you know, in your heart of hearts, that you must be. When all the reason, feeling, and logic in the entire world are stacked up against you, and yet some part of you still wants to walk away. You need to be alone whenever some quiet, gentle part of yourself suggests that now is not the time. Here is not the place. They are not the person. You need to be alone whenever you are trying to fit a square peg into a round hole, and it just won't twist in to fit. You need to be alone when you are lost. When you are found. When you are whole. When you are broken.

Someday, you'll understand that you can be all of those things alongside somebody else. But first and foremost, you need to learn to be them all alone.

14

WHY IT'S SO HARD TO GET OVER A CHEATER

It is hard to get over a cheater because when you leave the relationship, there are two people you must mourn. One is the asshole who cheated on you in all their flawed, unfaithful glory. This is the person it is easy to get mad at, the person it is easy to cut off contact with, the person it is easy to talk shit about while you're out for cocktails with your girlfriends at night. It's the person you are glad to be leaving because you know that you don't deserve their bullshit in your life.

The other person you must get over is the person you thought they were. The relationship you thought you had. The trust you so carefully built, not knowing that the foundation was made up of quicksand. It's not the cheater you are mourning at 4 a.m. when you come home from the bar alone and want to call them up to tell them they're forgiven; it is their intangibly perfect alter-ego. The one you built a life with. The one you poured your trust into. The one you thought would always be there until they weren't. You hate the person they turned into but love the person they were. Love the way things were. Love the memory of each blissfully ignorant day with them so fiercely that it tears you to pieces.

It is hard to get over a cheater because you never get the closure you need. You cannot reason your way to the cause of the cheating — and I strongly encourage you not to try. The back of your mind will only make up reasons that scathe you: you weren't funny enough, sexy enough, or enticing enough. You didn't pay enough attention. You didn't make enough time. With every magazine title screaming "Ways to please your lover!" and "How to not scare the good ones away," you begin to suspect that it was your fault they cheated, not theirs. You know logically this is not true, but it *feels* true. The harder you search for a reason, the more the truth evades you. A simple lapse in judgment doesn't seem like an adequate explanation for the hell that you've been put through. So you search for a bigger, better reason that is not there.

It's hard to get over a cheater because the only person you hate more than them is yourself. You hate yourself for falling for them. For investing in them. For turning a blind eye to every red flag that was a clue along the way. You scorn yourself for believing every lie they told and letting it all come to fruition. You hate yourself for not putting together the puzzle pieces that you were never actually holding.

It is hard to get over a cheater because we are seldom given the chance to properly mourn them. We are encouraged to feel every scathing emotion we can muster toward our unfaithful lovers, but we're told that we cannot still love them. Cannot miss them. Cannot mourn the loss of that love because we should be too angry to feel sadness. We are not given the chance to go through the regular process of grieving somebody who was once a significant part of our lives. And because we try to deny ourselves this process, we exemplify the pain. We feel ashamed for still loving them. Ashamed for still needing to grieve. Ashamed of not being ready to start over right away, even though we know we deserve so much better. Ashamed because it must make us weak to feel anything other than hatred.

It is hard to get over a cheater because the real person we have to forgive at the end of the day is ourselves. We have to forgive ourselves for missing the signs that we couldn't possibly have seen. For losing a game we never signed up to play. For having a perfectly natural connection with a person who turned out to not be who they said they were. We don't want to accept that bad things can happen to us without precedence.

That we can be fooled and treated unfairly and still end up the loser in the end. We want to believe in the eternal balance of the Universe, which suggests that when we are in pain we have done something wrong. It is hard to get over a cheater because it means accepting the bizarre notion that life can be unfair in the harshest sense of the word.

It is hard to get over a cheater because a betrayal of trust turns your world upside down. And the only way to flip it right-side up again is to give ourselves permission to work through it. To accept what happened. To mourn someone we hate. To grieve a relationship we walked away from. To work through every paradoxical situation we encounter until we come through on the other side. The side with a clean slate. The side where we don't just suspect that we deserve better—we *know*. And the side where we are proud of ourselves for never accepting any less.

15

READ THIS IF YOU FEEL LIKE IT'S TAKING YOU TOO LONG TO MOVE ON

Everybody seems to have a different rule about how long it should take you to get over something. If it's a relationship, they tell you half the length of it. If it's a loss, they tell you approximately a year—long enough to go through each special occasion when you're used to having them by your side. We use language like 'moving on' and 'letting go' as though they're actions as simple as shutting a door and physically walking away. We uncurl our fingers and drop whatever we are holding—that's letting go, right? That's all it takes?

I don't think I've experienced a single loss in my life that I've gotten over in the time frame that seems to have been allotted by society as 'acceptable.' And I suspect that I'm not alone there. It is not human nature to let go. We are, at our core, territorial creatures. We fight to hold onto what we love. Giving up isn't in any way instinctual.

If there's anything I wish we could talk more about, it's the in-between stages of letting someone go. Because nobody lets go in an instant. You let go once. And then you let go again. And then again and again and again. You let someone go at the grocery store when their favorite type of soup is on sale, and you don't buy it. You let them go again when you're cleaning your bathroom and have to throw out the bottle of body wash that smells like them. You let them go that night at the bar when you go home with somebody else, or you let them go every year on the anniversary of the day you lost them. Sometimes, you'll have to let one person go a thousand different times, a thousand different ways, and there's nothing pathetic or abnormal about that. You are human. And it isn't always as simple as making one decision and never looking back.

Moving on isn't always about speeding enthusiastically forward so much as it's about having one foot on the gas and the other on the brakes—releasing and accelerating in turn. You're not a failure for getting to someplace amazing and still feeling like a part of yourself is missing once you get there. You're not pathetic for mourning while you grow. The bad things don't disappear in the blink of an eye, and the good things don't spring up into existence without reigning at least a tiny bit of collateral damage. It takes time for everything to even out. And it should.

The truth is, none of us want to think of ourselves as works in progress. We want everything to happen instantaneously: Falling in love, falling out of it, letting go of what we know we ought to leave in the past, and moving on to whatever comes next. We hate the in-between spaces—the times when we're okay but not quite there yet. The periods where we suspect that growth is happening but have nothing to show for it. The days when everything feels like it's falling into place, and yet we still go home and cry into our pillow because there's nobody to share our good fortune with. If success is a staircase, we are eternally taking two steps forward and one step back, and that's okay. That's how we keep ourselves in check. It's how we keep ourselves from blowing the whole shebang.

We have to be patient with ourselves as we move through the parts in between where we've been and where we're going. We have to let the chasm motivate rather than dishearten us. It's okay to not be there yet. It's okay to be unsure of every step that you take forward. We don't talk about how moving on sometimes feels like we're fighting every part of our most basic instincts, but we should. We should talk about how growth is often every bit as painful as it is beautiful.

Because growth and letting go are so complexly intertwined that we often only see one or the other. We forget that they can exist side by side—releasing the old while letting in the new. We forget that we have the ability to do the exact same thing. And that if we'd only stop beating ourselves up over it, we might realize just how far we've already come.

16

HERE IS WHEN YOU'LL GET OVER YOUR EX

You'll get over your ex the first time you forget their Mom's birthday. It may hit you while you're doing groceries, four days prior to the date, or even weeks after it passes, but you'll suddenly identify the nagging feeling inside the back of your mind that there was something you'd forgotten about the date June seventeenth. It will shock you that your mind has jumped ahead in the process of moving on—dropping subtle memories it no longer has a use for and surreptitiously discarding any knowledge that stands between you and moving forward.

So you let the important dates pass—first a family member's birthday and then their birthday, then yours, and on some days, the distance seems impossibly small to bridge—the phone seems so easy to pick up, but you fight the urge and keep going. Some part of you knows better—that you have to wait this out. You have to take it in waves. You know that someday you'll forget their birthday and they'll forget yours too and until that day you keep yourself busy. You keep moving. And you keep letting the small details slide.

You'll get over your ex the first time you receive exciting news, and it doesn't occur to you to call them. When you cut your hair dramatically, do not think to send them a picture. When you finally land that dream job, you do not invite them to the celebratory happy hour. You will realize that at some point—perhaps during a long lapse of attention—your life has become only your own again. Your triumphs and failures belong to you in a way that is enticing, invigorating, and just the slightest bit sad all at once. But it doesn't make you want to run back to the past. You have grown comfortable in your autonomy, and it's somewhere you kind of want to stay.

You'll get over your ex when you meet someone new. Not when you hook up or shack up or even fall in love with another human being, but the first time you find yourself sitting across a crowded café table from someone whose smile melts you and whose arms you'd fit perfectly into, and yet some part of you is holding back. You'll realize at that moment that life has ceased to be a frantic dash to find someone who can replace your ex or fill the aching hole they left inside of you. You're putting your heart back together, and you want to do it properly before you jump feet-first into something new. You know that someday you will love someone else—that the capacity for affection and belonging is not lost on you and that you're not going to end up alone. You're not broken or hopeless or loveless just because your heart is aching—you are simply healing yourself. And when you're done, there will be a whole new world waiting for you.

You will not get over your ex all at once. You'll get over them through a series of tiny, tender moments that bring you quietly back to yourself. And in some ways, they'll never really leave you. The people who change us in those big, irrevocable ways never do. To get over them, we'd have to alter ourselves into people so unrecognizable that we'd lose who we are in the process. And so instead, we learn to integrate the influence they had—the books you now read because of topics that they turned you on to. The music you now download because of the lyrics they loved. The ways you now look at the world that would never have occurred to you if they had not opened your eyes up to seeing and doing things differently. We don't ever lose people we love in their entirety, and perhaps we never should—we become bigger, more encompassing people ourselves because of it.

You'll get over your ex the day you realize that you damn well may never get over them. That pieces of them will live on inside you forever and that discarding them would mean discarding parts of yourself. But the day that you get to move on is the day you simply decide to do so despite it—despite the tired, restless ache that begs you not to take a chance. Despite the fearful, self-conscious mind that tells you nobody will ever love you better. Despite every careless part of you that wants to keep holding on but knows that it needs to let go. The day when you finally move on is the day you decide to move forward—with all of your fear, all your pain, and all your subtle hesitations. It's the day you finally get over yourself.

17

WHAT THEY DON'T TELL YOU ABOUT LOVE

They don't tell you that you'll spend much of your adult life trying to reconstruct your first experience of love. That for a while, every date, every relationship, and every person you fall into lust with will continuously be held to the impossible standard of the first person who ever made a home inside your heart, and that everyone else will fall short. They don't tell you that first love is a rampant, insatiable beast and that someday you'll be glad you've found something more tame. But for a while, you'll miss the wilderness. And that's okay.

They don't tell you that love is addicting. That it has the inexplicable potential to consume every part of your being and make you forget what you once wanted in its absence. That you will not always be ready for the world love sweeps you away to and that you'll lose your own mind and your footing in ways you swore you never would. They don't tell you that your first hit of love is every bit as potent as your first hit of cocaine and that it's a wholly unsustainable addiction.

They don't tell you that love will be work. That it won't always be a freely flowing stream of adoration and attention and growth. That sometimes love will mean choices you don't want to make and roads you don't want to take, and that it's going to be every bit as unglamorous as it is incredible and brave. They don't tell you that love might turn you into someone you don't want to be. And that you're going to have to do a lot of learning if you ever want to grow inside of love.

They don't tell you that love is going to break you. That someday, every idealistic hope you once had about what it means to give and receive love freely will be shattered in a way you can never fully reconstruct. That no matter how many hearts and hands and futures you hold with someone else after this point, you'll never get back to the way you once looked at love and hoped that it would manifest for you. They don't tell you that this will eventually be a good thing—that the real, concrete love will ultimately overshadow the flimsy, fantasy love you'd constructed in your mind. But that getting there is going to be a trip. One you'll be wholly unprepared to make and may never entirely heal from.

They don't tell you that you'll forget to be loved. That at some point in the process of reaching and striving and growing and always moving forward in your life, you'll let love slide by the wayside. That you'll subtly forget what it's like to be touched, to be treasured, to be adored and admired by another human being with a mind and a body every bit as real as yours. They don't map out the dull, inconsolable ache that grows inside of you the longer you let yourself forget that you're desiring love. They don't tell you that you need it like water and air and that no matter how hard you try to prove the opposite, a tiny part of you will always be unfulfilled without it.

They don't tell you that love is a habit. That you can fall out of it and become clumsy and awkward and unpracticed at giving and accepting it back. That you will grow impatient with yourself in the process, wondering why on earth the walls around your heart have risen so high since you last knocked them down. That some old wounds will bleed again at every tender touch and that it's going to take a while to heal them. They don't tell you that love can be forgotten until suddenly, unexpectedly, it's not. They don't tell you that once you start back up, love becomes the most impossible habit to break.

They don't tell you that nobody can tell you the way love is going to feel for you. That it's an experience so unique to all of us that we'll never fully understand what we're getting ourselves into until we find ourselves right in the middle of it. They don't tell you that it will be loud and quiet, big and small, fierce and unassuming, proud and shameful, all at once. They don't tell you what love will end up meaning to you because they can't.

Because for some things, we still have no words.

18

JUST BE THE ONE WHO CARES MORE

Somebody always has to care more.

This is the unfortunate cardinal rule of how relationships function. If one person didn't care a teeny bit more than the other, no one would ever get asked out. Or proposed to. Or counseled back from the brink of divorce. Someone always has to put in a tiny bit more effort than the other party is offering. Throughout the course of your life, you're going to be on both sides of the situation at least once.

You're going to be loved by someone who you just kind of like. You're going to be head over heels for someone who essentially thinks you're okay. And I can almost entirely assure you that you're going to loathe the latter situation. We all do. Being the one who cares more makes you feel uncomfortably desperate—like you suddenly have to justify your entire existence to somebody else.

"I'm a catch!" You'll want to shout at them. "I'm smart and adorable, my jokes are well-timed, and my hair looks fantastic today." You'll comb through possible reasons why they are not as ethereally pumped about you as you are about them, and you'll come up empty-handed at best, filled with self-doubt at worst. You will resolve to care less. You will strive to inhibit the most basic emotional response possible to a situation that you are happy about.

And you know what? That is bullshit.

Being the one who cares less makes us feel cool and suave. But never anything more than that. It can't even begin to compare with the excitement of meeting someone you are CRAZY about. Someone who lights up your day with every subtle interaction. Someone you cannot wait to see again. Someone you suddenly want to spend every waking moment with, even if that's crazy and impulsive and happening way too fast. I know it's a trial to be the one who cares more. But it's also the most enthralling, fulfilling feeling, and I urge you not to sell yourself short of it.

Just be the freaking person who cares more. Be the person who tries harder, loves stronger, and gives more of a shit than all of the half-alive people who surround them. Be the person who answers their messages, shows up to their commitments, and doesn't leave others hanging or guessing at their eternally vague intentions. Be the person you wish you were dating. If you're sick of the game, then stop playing it. If you're tired of the bullshit, then cut it.

Because the last thing this world needs is one more indifferent person. If you're the only one left with passion, then use it. Use the hell out of it. At the end of your life, go out with a bruised-up, worn-out heart that gave too much love, loved too intensely, and felt too fiercely. Go out with the certainty that you gave it everything you had and didn't hold anything back. Go out empty-handed when it comes to should-haves and might-have-beens. Because it's an infinitely more fulfilling way to live than the alternative. It will always be more honorable to be out in the field getting trampled on than to be on the sidelines feeling superior for never having tried.

I am tired of taking pride in being the one who cares less. It's not a badge of honor to wear on your chest as a triumph of human detachment. If you care less, cut the cord. If you care more, then show it. Answer your messages. Show up to your commitments. Don't scale back or water down your passion to keep up with someone dead inside. Arrive with enthusiasm to every waking moment of your life.

Because that is what we need in this world—more people who care. More people who give a shit. More people who aren't afraid to shout what they want from the rooftops and pursue it with a sense of abandon. We need more people with passion. More people with gusto. More people who will stand up and fight for exactly what they want out of life because they aren't afraid to look a little stupid and feel a little disappointed on their way to achieving what they want out of it.

We need more people who care more, regardless of how that makes them look. More people who are, perhaps, precisely like you.

19

TAKE A CHANCE ON ME

Take a chance on me.

I know those words are wrought with uncertainty. I know you've taken chances before, and they have flopped and floundered and left you high and dry. I know you are scared to start again after everything before this has failed you—I am, too. But baby, if I have to fail again, it is you I want to go down in flames with. I know that nothing ever works out, but if it does, it would be this. It would be here. It would be you and me and whatever this fire is between us.

Take a chance on me. Because the timing's always going to be wrong and the stars are never going to align, but I would break every clock in this city. I'd stop every star from shining if it meant that, for one afternoon, we could cast all that aside and give in. Give in to the complete impossibility that something could work here despite everything that stands in the way. Give in to how your touch makes me shiver, and your words make my mind race and reel. Give in to the improbability that this is going to work out or end well or fall into place exactly as we'd hoped or that any of it will be even half worth it in the end. Give in to senselessness. Give in to you, finally giving in to me.

Take a chance on me—because tomorrow, the Universe could collapse in on itself. This city could disintegrate to ashes, and the sun could burst into a thousand disjointed rays. I'll be damned if I am going to die without knowing what it feels like to have your lips on mine. Because when the end comes, you could be at work filing papers, and I could be sipping a latte at the coffee shop, and your last thought could be, "This paper won't—" and mine could be, "What a delicious dr—." But when that blinding flash of light emerges and our last moments on earth splinter senselessly, I want to remember the way you laughed right into my mouth while you kissed me and the feeling of your skin against mine.

Take a chance on me because no chance ever works out. Because every relationship seems to end in heartbreak, and every new beginning eventually reaches a conclusion, but we have all of the time in the world between those two points, and I intend to enjoy every second. Because someday I might hate the way you squint when you're concentrating, and you might despise the way I pace when I'm nervous, but right now, you are perfect and endearing and pure, and why shouldn't we enjoy that? Because everything ends eventually, and the whole point is to love what's in between, and if, for me, that gets to be you, then I am happy.

Take a chance on me, even though I cannot promise it will be worth it. I have no guarantees, crystal ball, or vision of the future where we're happy and healthy and together for the rest of our days. I have been promised too many forevers to have much faith in them anymore, so instead, I'd like to offer you right now. I can offer you only this moment, where I'm standing in front of you, knowing all of this may someday fall apart, but that someday is not what I'm looking for anymore. I have right here and right now, and all I can hope is that that is enough. That we can figure out the future as it comes.

Take a chance on me—because I want to take a chance on you.

And it only has to work out once.

20

WHAT WE FORGET WHEN WE SAY THE TIMING'S WRONG

Let's talk about how our timing's off.

You see, we couldn't have planned this out worse.

It would have been infinitely easier to meet you two years earlier, three years later, in a different space, place, country, or time zone.

It would have been simpler to meet you in a world where I could wake up nestled tightly beside you, and you could join in each adventure I took on.

It would be marvelous to have all our fates aligned and to see the timing play itself out flawlessly.

But I'm inclined to say we ought to count our blessings.

Because here's the absolute miracle that we cannot allow ourselves to ignore: out of the billions of years that earth has existed, you and I ended up alive at the exact same time.

I wasn't born on your 90th birthday. You didn't die an untimely death at age 3.

I didn't live as a pauper in the year 400 B.C. You will not spring into existence 500 years into the future. Out of all the centuries, eras, time periods, and Universes we could have ended up in, we somehow both ended up here.

We ended up in the era with planes and trains and cars and cell phones and Skype calls. We ended up in the age of relentless communication and instantaneous connection. Of all the possible worlds we could have gotten stuck in, we found ourselves living in a time when it's possible to wake up to a good morning text every day from someone clear across the world.

And when you look at it that way, it doesn't seem so bad. When you look at it that way, it doesn't seem unbearable to wait for a couple more months or a few painstaking years or a single stretch of absence that will eventually be bridged. When you look at it from the angle of the bleak improbability that two people like you and I would ever co-exist, the timing doesn't seem so wrong at all.

Because really, who are you and I to demand any more from the Universe? Who are we to mandate that the stars align in our favor and the fortunes always cater to our fates? When we chisel it down to probability, we've already come out on top here. So it's only fair we put in some work.

Because the truth about the timing being wrong is that it's nothing more than the world's flimsiest reason not to try.

It's the simplest excuse to pack it in. It's a pre-designed reason to bow out. Saying that the timing is wrong is saying nothing more than *'You aren't worth any inconvenience.'*

And when it comes to you, that is untrue.

When it comes to you, I'd wade through limitless eras and time zones and alternate realities and Universes trying to find you.

I'd wait for decades or ages or centuries or lifetimes. I'd wait through wars and resolutions and tsunamis and ice ages and apocalypses. I'd wait indefinitely. I'd wait forever.

But the brilliant thing is, I don't have to do any of that. Because here we are right now. At this time. In this Universe.

And as long as you're alive here and I'm alive too, the timing is right enough for me.

21

LET ME FALL IN LOVE WITH YOUR DARKNESS

Please stop trying to sell me your perfection.

You are flawed, and I'm flawed, and we're both wearing shiny cloaks of virtue, but I know that when the day is done and the lights are dimmed, you shed all your sainthood like snakeskin, and I do, too. Tell me what you're hiding, what you're harboring, what you don't want the world to know about yourself for fear that it will be cast into light.

Tell me about the times you couldn't save yourself. Give me your broken parts, your fractured pieces, everything that's weighed too heavily on the floor of your heart for you to ever reach down and reassemble. Tell me where you went the first time that you lost yourself. Tell me the ways in which you never came back. Give me a map with coordinates that lead into the deepest, most twisted corner of your soul where all of your unconquered demons still lurk. Let me see them. Let me reach out and touch them with my own trembling fingers because I still can't bear to face my own.

Give me your shortcomings. Tell me the story of the first person you never became and all the ways in which you let him die. Tell me which regrets tear your heartstrings and which unfulfilled dreams still take up residence under your skin. Show me the mountains you never conquered, the roads you never traversed, the battles you surrendered before ever setting foot upon enemy soil. Show me the things you never measured up to because there's no war more wounding than the one we never waged, and there's no road more daunting than the one we never walked down.

Give me your struggles and impurities. Tell me about the worst thing you have ever done. Tell me about the regret that slithered under your skin and beat through your bloodstream like an unwelcome disease after you made the biggest mistake of your life. Tell me how it ripped straight into your soul and took you over. Talk to me about the times you couldn't look at yourself in the mirror or fall asleep at night because the malevolence and madness of your own mind kept you reeling. Give me your vices and misjudgments because I can match each one with my own. Tell me all the ways in which you're scarred by your own capacity for darkness.

Let me fall in love with your human parts—the battles you can't fight, the wounds you can't heal, all the ways in which you are not enough for yourself. Give me your joys and your pain in equal measure because you are the most brilliant and terrible mixture of both.

I don't want your good intentions and your well wishes. I want the whole of you, the depth of you, the breadth of all you are, and the light that shines in between your broken parts. Let me fall in love with what you're missing, what you've lost, and what you're still holding onto, through and despite all of it. Show me the things you haven't lost along the way. And I will show you your own greatest strengths.

22

I FLAT-OUT REFUSE TO MARRY ANYONE UNLESS THESE ARE OUR VOWS

Marrying you is not the end of my liberty; it's the beginning of it.

You're the person I want to dive headfirst into life with. When I go out on the weekends, it is you I want shutting down the club with me. When I plan an adventure, it is you I want holding the map. When I speculate about the future, I want to see you in every outlandish fantasy I plan for myself. You're the person I want to rant excitedly to over happy hour drinks. You're the person I want to dance around the house in my underwear with. You're the person who makes the whole world feel wide open to me, and I want to take advantage of that. I want to plunge into the future with you—because it looks bigger and brighter by your side than I ever could have imagined.

I don't want to settle down with you. I want to take off with you—to far-away countries, foreign landscapes, gems, and corners of the world that would only have looked half as amazing without you by my side. When I strap on a backpack and head to the airport, I want you to be boarding that plane with me. You're the person I want to get lost with, set up camp with, stumble through dark streets with at 5 a.m. after a long, rambunctious night in a city that we can't pronounce the name of. When I get home and have tale after ridiculous tale to recite to my friends, you're the one I want there to back up my claims. You're the person I want to come home to and the person I want to escape with. I want you on every adventure I take for the rest of my life. I want to do everything on earth with you.

I don't want to be the person you always agree with. I want to be the person you challenge—to change, grow, and expand in ways that never occurred to me before I met you. I want heated debates at 3 a.m. I want stark disagreements when I'm acting out of line. I want passionate arguments about the way we're living because your fire fuels mine, and I never want that spark to die out. I want to be someone you aren't afraid to challenge because sometimes I need that extra push. And you can bet your ass that I'll push you right back.

I don't want to let myself go now that I have you—I want to build myself up alongside you. Something about you inspires me to be bigger, brighter, bolder than I ever knew that I could become. And I hope that I inspire you, too. That together, we can encourage one another to grow into the fullest, strongest, fiercest versions of each other. That ten years from now, we will be prouder than ever to be standing beside one another, and that twenty years later, we'll be even prouder still. I hope you're not expecting to grow stagnant in love because something about you makes me feel like my best self on steroids, and I do not plan to let that feeling die.

If there's anything I am not worried about, it's us falling apart. The truth is I never fell in love with you anyway; I walked into love—assuredly, deliberately, and without a backward glance. I chose you from the first day I met you, and baby, I promise to keep choosing you. Through every fight, I'll choose you. Through every temptation, I'll choose you. Through every twist and bump in the road that threatens to tear us apart, I will choose you with the ferocious certainty I've felt since the first time I ever laid eyes on you. I'm not worried about falling out of love with you, baby, because I never fell in. Loving you was a waking, conscious choice, and it's one that I'm going to keep making until the day my heart stops beating.

Now, let's stop with these frivolous vows—there's a party to have! We have gifts to tear open, champagne to chug, and a whirlwind honeymoon to embark on. This whole marriage thing is old and tired, but we most certainly are not. After all, you're only young and wild once. And baby, our wildest days are just beginning.

23

WHAT THE BEGINNING OF A RELATIONSHIP FEELS LIKE AFTER THE END OF SO MANY OTHERS

After a certain amount of time, there is a rhythm to falling in love.

You meet someone. You fall mercilessly for them. And it works—for a while. You carve out those memories—the ones that seem so unique to just you and that one other person: The way they'd kiss you with firm hands and eyes open. The highway that you'd drive down with the windows down and the radio cranked. The way they'd wrap their arms around you at night that made you feel as though the entire world was safe and serene for just a moment. You fall easily into the tranquility of combining your moments with somebody else's because it feels like you can trust it this time. Like it is going to be okay. Like you can stay there.

Except you never can. It's not always planned or deliberate. It's not always harsh or malicious. But some inhuman part of us seems programmed to fall apart, and at one point or another, it always does.

You wake up one too many mornings with the right side of the bed lying empty. You get busy with your day and respond less frequently to your text messages. And eventually, the big kicker comes. A job in another city. A communication breakdown. A compromise that perhaps you would both like to make but refuse to. There are too many principles guiding us that surmount basic emotion, and so we let them break us apart. We learn to be alone again. And it's not so bad, after all—we can depend on ourselves, we can plan our own futures, we can live our lives wholly and selfishly without having to worry about who we are harming.

Until it all begins again. You go out to dinner with someone whose smile lights up your evening, whose touch makes you shiver, and whose thoughts keep you wide awake and reeling through the nighttime. And it's beautiful and perfect and genuine, except you can't help but remember that the beginning necessitates the end.

That someday, this person who lights up your existence may also be the person you abhor—the one you throw from your life and block from your Facebook feed and cringe at the mention of their name. That someday, everything you love about this person may also be the thing that you hate. Their unassuming laugh will become unbearably annoying. Their innate library of knowledge will seem condescending and dry. The words and phrases that take you off guard now will someday be a puzzle you're tired of putting together. You could hate this person every bit as much as you love them, and you're not sure if the risk will be worth it. They text you on a lazy Sunday evening while you're watching TV, and you're not sure what you ought to text them back.

"Do you think that we should really start this up?" You want to ask them. "What if I eventually hate you? What if you fall out of love? What if every quirk we admire about one another becomes tired and wearisome as this goes on? What if my effervescent wit becomes manipulative and meddlesome with time? What if your calculating nature grows exhausting? What if we cease to enthrall each other? What if I become one more thing you can shrug off with detached indifference?"

You want to ask these deadpan questions, but you know that the most important ones are those that you ought to be asking yourself.

Will you regret this? Will it come back to haunt you? Four years from now, will you wish that you could travel back to this exact moment in time and put the phone down? Let the message go unanswered, let the love go undiscovered, let every fearful, exhilarating step you could take towards this person go untraveled? Will you know with such clarity, at a much later point in time, that none of this is worth the pain that it will someday evoke?

And if you knew the answer to all of it, would you answer the text anyway?

Because maybe it's not always about the endgame—as painful and debilitating as it can be. What if your future self could travel back in time and tell your current self that the end would be every bit as excruciating as you fear but that you should answer that text message anyway? That you should take that leap. That the relationship you're going to enter into is going to teach you more about love, the world, and yourself than you could ever imagine. That it's going to be worth every ounce of the pain. That love always is.

What if you knew that the person you would fall in love with would someday be the utterly wrong person for you but that right now, they are precisely what you need? What if it doesn't have to last forever? What if that's not the point at all?

Maybe we have an endless, unrestricted amount to learn from one another. Maybe we have no reason not to jump into every new relationship, every possibility, every chance we come across to grow bigger and bolder through love, whether it works out or not. Maybe it's just a matter of being brave enough to take that chance. To answer that text message. To let it start all over again.

Because maybe the end game is worth it every time. Maybe the heartbreak is a side effect of something so brilliant that it eventually overshadows the destruction. Maybe some things don't have to last forever in order to change you irrevocably. And once you've loved enough people, maybe that's exactly what you know—that you're strong enough to survive it. Strong enough to change from it. And strong enough and brave enough to choose the potential for growth over the fear of getting hurt every time.

24

PLEASE DELETE MY NUMBER

Because I'm going to miss you. Because you're going to pop into my mind on a rainy Sunday evening when Bon Iver is humming in the background, and I've poured myself a tall glass of wine, and a whiff of your old cologne catches me suddenly off guard—lingering in the apartment like an unwanted house guest who was never invited to stay.

Please delete my number. Because I'm going to want to call you when I apply for that job you always said that I should go for, or cut my hair in the way I never dared to, or get that dog we always talked about getting and don't know who to text its eager picture to. I'm going to want to call you when the Bills win, when the last snow melts, and when each long, wine-saturated night draws to a close, and I wish that it were still you I was on my way home to.

Please delete my number—because I didn't want to end up here. Because the word "Maybe" is the slowest form of torture that you possibly could have settled on, dragging out a hope that died long ago despite your stark refusal to bury it. Because *maybe* doesn't mean, "This may happen."

It means, "I am too fearful to go but not strong enough to stay."

It means, "I'll miss you, but not enough to be with you."

It means, "I love you, but not quite enough to stick around and fight."

Please delete my number—because I don't want to delete you. Because I want you with a certainty that you will perhaps never possess. Because I do not have to think twice about whether I would like to answer your text messages or pick up your phone calls. Because I'm sure. Because I do not love people halfway, and that's where you and I differ. I don't want the occasional phone call. I don't want to play your tired-out game.

Please delete my number because I'm not going to settle for your maybes. I want concrete. I want definite. I want people who call when they say they will and show up when they plan to. I don't want to spend my life waiting, wasted on someone who can only love halfway. I do not want your texts, late at night, that say,

"I miss you" or

"I'm sorry" or

"I just need a little bit more time."

Please delete my number—because I'm deleting yours. And you can find someone new to text your maybes to.

25

HERE IS HOW YOU STOP WAITING FOR SOMEONE TO COME BACK

You stop waiting for them to come back by becoming profoundly uncomfortable. You move through the places where you wish they still were, and you hold your own hand as you go. You don't lie to yourself about how it is going to be easy and happy and new in a way that is wonderful—not yet. First, you delve right into the deepest part of the dark, murky water of missing them, and you let it envelop you. You feel their absence on a core, guttural level. You absorb it in exactly the way that you're afraid of. You let it sink under your skin.

You stop waiting for them by letting things change. You cut your hair and know they'll never see it. You quit your job and know you'll never tell them about the new one. You let people into your life that you know they'll never get the chance to love or hate or sit up at night discussing with you. You allow the delicate pattern of the life you'd built with them to dissipate and change form with the arrival of each new twist. You aren't okay with it, so you let it not be okay. You brace yourself each time for the impact. You know that someday, change will come naturally again, and even that feels sort of sad.

You stop waiting by being vulnerable with someone new. You start giving your secrets away—the ones you thought were safe with them until suddenly they weren't. You realize that knowing you deeply isn't an experience that was exclusive to them, and you let that be as surprising as it is disheartening. You let new forms of intimacy enter your life, and you allow them to feel unnatural for a while.

You stop waiting for them to come back by realizing that pain is an inevitable component of moving forward. You stop waiting for the chasm in your heart to close up, and you take whatever steps you need to on trembling, uncertain legs. You realize that sometimes, that's truly the only way to move forward: sadly and uncertainly and long before you are ready. That if you wait until you feel ready, you may just be waiting forever.

You stop waiting for someone to come back by choosing to go forward without them. And perhaps this is the saddest, most straightforward truth—that we must deliberately move ourselves away from the people we have loved and lost, or else we will stay lost alongside them. That forward, alone, may not be the most desirable option, but it is the only one we have. And we don't get to trade in our hand.

The truth about ceasing to wait for someone is that eventually, someday, someone else has to show up to fill his or her place. And that person has to be you. You have to show up to your new life, your new world, and your new way of doing things, no matter how painful and raw it all feels. You have to face forward toward the future you hadn't planned for and the life you didn't know that you would lead. You have to stop showing up to the land of used-to-bes and could-be-stills and show up to this world. The one where it hurts. The one that's unfair. The world that is here because it's the only one you have left.

You stop waiting for someone to come back through a series of slow, deliberate steps that move you away from the life you thought you'd have and towards the one waiting for you. It's the life that shows up once you make the conscious, uncomfortable decision to leave the past behind. To learn from the people you've lost and to embrace the people that you have left. To embrace the life you have left. And to bring yourself back to it as fully and wholly as you wish that you could bring back someone else.

26

MAYBE YOU AND I DON'T GET ANOTHER UNIVERSE

We all love the Theory Of Multiple Universes.

We loved it when William James coined it. We loved the sparks of debate that followed after. We love entertaining the idea that this is not the only world we're stuck with and that there are infinite alternatives out there.

We love the theory of multiple universes because it allows us to believe that all the people we didn't become, all the roads we didn't take, all the times we turned left when we should have turned right, didn't wither and die a senseless death. We like to believe that somewhere out there, there's a Universe where we get to have made the other choice. The one that might have changed us. Grown us. Made us into bigger, braver people than the ones who we became instead.

These other hypothetical universes allow us so many leniencies. They are where we can go to unload our hearts and our failures and regrets. *In some Universe, these choices are not mine. In some lifetime, I did it all better.*

I used to believe that there were so many Universes for you and I.

There was the one where we held it together. The one where we stuck around, worked it out, ironed out our heartbreaks, and forgave one another for it all.

There was the one where there was nothing to forgive—where we grew up as slowly as we needed to, never had to turn against each other, didn't have greater ambitions or wandering eyes or weary, mismatched hopes clasped too tightly to our chests. One where everything happened the way it was supposed to.

There was the one where it was simpler, easier, pure. The one where we wanted the same things, laughed at the same jokes, and loved each other's families as if they were our own. Where my ambitions didn't push you out of the picture and where your insipid lack of confidence didn't tear us apart at the seams. In that Universe, we have cats. I seem like more of a cat person in that Universe.

I have driven myself mad over the years, mapping out all these Universes for you and I. If-only this. What-if-I'd that. Tracing and trailing through our history, there are so many moments where our galaxies split in half. Where our stars realigned, and our planets shifted swiftly, and we found ourselves on wildly different courses than the ones we should have taken.

But we don't live in any of those Universes.

We live in this one, the one where we lost each other.

And this has been the hardest Universe to swallow.

Out of all possible Universes, we landed in the one that broke us. The one where two halves did not make a whole and every molehill turned into a mountain. This is the Universe where, in ten hundred thousand tiny ways, we were wrong for each other. It's the one where we're always going to be.

I think that so many lovers get those alternate Universes where they are happier and freer and more fulfilled by each other's side. But I like to think we don't get one. I like to think that no matter which roads we'd taken, which decisions we'd made, which errors of judgment we'd reversed, there isn't a Universe out there that could possibly have saved us.

I want us to be that single glitch in the matrix. I want it to all be far out of our control.

Because the thing about loving you is that I'd have waded through an infinite number of Universes trying to find the one that's right for us. The one that would have suited us, strengthened us, let us be the partners we needed to be for each other.

But there are too many galaxies out there. There are too many fractures, too many splinters, too many moments where the roads diverged and the manifestations of our choices split into ten thousand alternate lives. There are enough what-ifs out there for me to get lost in forever, and I don't want to spend my time chasing our cosmos anymore.

I'm ready to come back to this Universe.

I'm ready to accept that there may not be another Universe out there for us. And maybe that's okay.

There's still Universe enough here for me.

And maybe this is the Universe where I learn to not need you anymore.

27

WHEN YOU HAVE TO LEAVE THE BEST THINGS BEHIND

We're not always going to be ready for the changes life presents us with.

There will be times when we get to stay exactly where we're happy—curled up in the lap of everything we want, everything we have, and everything we're comfortable with. There will be times when we struggle—grasping to figure things out and get to wherever we're going next. And perhaps the most challenging time of all will be the chasm that exists between these times—when something unexpectedly rips what we want from us and forces us to leave it behind. When we have to walk away before we're ready. When we have to leave what we want and what we love in the past.

There's nothing more difficult than walking away from what we love before we're ready to. Even when every fiber of our being understands that we must go, we want to stay. We want to linger. We want to find a loophole or shortcut that allows us to have it all. We forget that there's a future. Some incorrigible part of us so easily forgets that there are good things ahead. Better things ahead, even. And perhaps that's what we need to understand the most fully when we're facing those times of transition—that all our best moments aren't all behind us.

We have to believe that there are so, so many better things coming than any of the things we have left in the past. You have to have faith in the future, in the unknown, in the tomorrows and somedays that will line up in ways you can't possibly imagine from where you're standing now. You have to have faith in yourself—faith that you will get yourself to where you want to go, even if you're not entirely certain where that is yet. Faith that your future self will figure it out. Faith that you are going to fight for yourself as determinately and as passionately as you deserve to be fought for, no matter where you're headed next.

You have to remember every dreary day that preceded the best days of your life and realize that that's where you are right now—in the middle of that rainy day when it seems like everything is going wrong. You weren't at the end of the story back then, and you're not at the end of the story now. Just because the scene in the rearview mirror looks nicer than the scene on the road ahead doesn't mean you'll never reach another beautiful destination. It just means you're not there yet.

When you're leaving behind a place or a person or a period of time when you were happy, you have to take yourself back to the start. You have to remember how unexpectedly you found so many of the things that ended up changing your life—how seemingly randomly the cards were stacked right before they unfolded the way they did.

You have to remember that the Universe is infinitely more chaotic than we give it credit for—that there are people you're going to meet who you couldn't dream up if you tried. That there are situations you'll encounter that you never would have pictured yourself experiencing. That there will be days bursting with more happiness and light than you could possibly fathom from where you're standing now. You have to think of all the times that life has surprised you for the better and know that it can do it again. That it will do it again—as long as you stay open to those changes. As long as you don't let the endings close you off from the new beginnings waiting ahead.

It's rare, and it's wonderful to ever find a place, person, or certain situation that makes you want to linger for longer. We are creatures of the past and the future—always mourning what we've done or gunning fearlessly towards what comes next. When happiness hits us, we all want to cling to it as tightly and mercilessly as possible. We want to capture it and hold it between our palms forever—not realizing that we have to let it go for it to mean anything at all. That we have to keep moving onward, facing forward, steering constantly into the fearful and unknown. That all the best moments of our lives are still waiting for us on the other side.

When we have to leave the things we love behind, we are allowed to mourn them. To miss them. To look back on them dejectedly and sadly. But we must never, ever forget that the best days of our lives are not all behind us. That there are more beautiful things awaiting us in the future than we could ever even fathom. That so many of our happiest days are still ahead. And that we have to keep moving to get there—no matter how tempting that view in that rearview mirror is. The future we want will not arrive without our participation. And in order to get there, we have to blindly and blissfully trust that it's going to be somewhere indescribably worth going.

28

WHAT IF I WON YOU BACK?

What if I showed up in your driveway on the eve of your twenty-fifth birthday with a boom box in my hands, my heart on my sleeve, and the words you always needed to hear no longer lodged inside my throat? What if you ran outside to meet me, and I versed you brash soliloquies of everything I could never say when we were lying beside one another, too afraid that one wrong word or strange movement could make it all come tumbling down? What if you listened? What if you took me in your arms and kissed me with the raw determination that you had at eighteen years old when we were still so goddamned shy around each other that we weren't sure if we'd ever find a way to come together? What if we started all over again, right there in that driveway?

What if you'd never left? What if we still lived in that bachelor apartment with the sink hanging over the toilet and the knobby, skittish motions of our bodies never quite fitting into the space we'd carved out for one other? What if the zealous old landlady ruled over the building, spoiling evenings with her half-deciphered rants about salvation and redemption and the brimstone that awaits those of us who don't believe? What if we believed in each other? What if I plotted out mistakes I've made over the years, and when I stopped thinking of you, there was an army of tiny, crooked lines drawn out in the sand? What if I told you I was sorry? What if you came home each evening to the TV turned up to the volume you like, with your favorite dinner waiting on the table, and your parents chatting with me through the other long end of the phone because I had decided to try? What if I changed for you? What if you changed for me, too?

What if, in a strange twist of fate, we both ended up with amnesia? What if we forgot everything about each other—all our names and birthdays and secrets and failures and triumphs, like that movie where Jim Carrey had to hide under his mother's kitchen table in his PJs, hoping his mind would never catch up? What if my eye caught yours at the grocery store, walking by the section with the olives that you always had to buy, and you caught me wrinkling my nose with disgust, and you found that endearing instead of frustrating again? What if you asked for my name? What if I told you what it was?

What if you took me on a date—sweet and simple, at that old Italian bistro that we always used to love? What if my laughter felt familiar on your lips, what if my body curved too simply into yours, what if our minds failed to remember, but our hands never forgot what it once meant to touch one another? What if it was stranger than we'd ever experienced but simpler than we ever could have dreamed?

What if we started again from the beginning—every first time, every slip-up, every speed bump that we hit along the way? What if we tried this time? What if we turned left at every place we once turned right? What if we fought through every bout we once gave up on? What if we screamed at one another so fervidly that all the neighbors flicked on their lights and paced outside our doorway with concern, yet we still chose to stay every time? What if my hand clasped yours on our fifty-third wedding anniversary, and I knew there was no better decision I could have made than spending my entire life loving you? What if we made it? What if our story lasted a lifetime and became the whole title of the book?

Or what if I'm wrong?

What if I knew, from the second you walked out the door, that there's only one ending to this story? What if we tried all there was left to try and we found that no boom box, no amnesia, or crazy twist of fate would be enough to save us now? What if I let you go?

What if we went on with our lives and were happy and fulfilled and sometimes lost within the chaos of it all, but one thing that we never got to hold onto was each other? What if we found we didn't need to? What if we someday discovered a kind of incomprehensible happiness that we never even thought to try for? What if our lives were only meant to intersect for just long enough to create the contrast we needed to go on living the rest of it? What if our hands gripped someone else's weathered hands at the end of our incredible lives and re-lived memories we couldn't possibly dream up from the place where we're standing right now?

What if I never won you back?

And what if—as much as we'd hate to admit it—that was the happiest ending of all?

29

HOW TO LOVE SOMEONE YOU CANNOT HOLD ONTO

We have all fallen for temporary people.

They come as swiftly as they go from our lives, with their reeling minds and striking bodies and genuine, wide-open hearts. They are hurricanes and madness and wrecking balls; they're sunshine and blissful surrenders.

We want to shelter ourselves from the storms that these people embody, but we also want to walk right into the center of them. We want their chaos and their madness; we want it the way others once wanted ours.

We are advised not to fall for these people. And yet we do, knowing full well we can't keep them. How could we not, after all?

We want their nows and forevers. We want their sleepy half-smiles over coffee every morning and their sturdy arms to lull us to sleep. We want their wine-drunk Saturday evenings and their lazy Sunday mornings. We want their words and their silences, their downfalls, and their strengths. We want the whole of the people we love, but we're sometimes only given a fraction. And so here's what we do with that instead.

When we don't get to hold on to the people we love, we wrap their memories in between our heartstrings, and we carry them with us. We remember the lilt of their laughter on the days when the rain comes pouring down. We envision the curves of their skin when we need to know that all is not lost. We take the moments we share with these people, and we freeze them, we immortalize them, we keep them preserved and alive inside the ancient museums of our minds.

Because love doesn't need to last forever to make a lasting impression.

We don't need to curse and resent and forget the people life didn't let us hold onto. We don't have to rid ourselves of their impressions and shelter ourselves from their impact. We're allowed to let them in. We're allowed to let them matter. We're allowed to engage in the temporary foolishness of falling for someone who is not going to be left holding our crippled, wrinkled hand fifty years down the road.

Because some people simply are not meant to stay forever. Some people come into our lives for a season, for a reason, for the simple purpose of showing us the world in a way we would never have seen it otherwise.

And what else can we do but hold onto these people while we have them?

What else do we do but grow enchanted by the brilliance of their minds, by the purity of their spirits, by the strength and intensity and contrast that they cast into the colorless corners of our lives?

What else do we do but memorize the scent of their skin, the taste of their bodies, and the wisdom of their ever-reeling mind, so long as we still have them captured inside the tangible corners of our Universe? What else do we do but love them with everything we have before they're gone?

After all, we never know how much time's left. Maybe anyone worth knowing is worth knowing for only a short while. Maybe anyone worth loving is worth loving inconclusively.

And when you look at it that way, it doesn't seem quite so unbearable at all: to allow yourself to love someone with everything you've got—and then to fully and completely let them go.

30

THIS IS ME LETTING YOU GO

This is me accepting that you're leaving. It's my acknowledgment that there's no further argument to make, no angle left to take, no plea or bargain I could wager that could get you to change your mind and stay. This is my subtle resignation to our downfall. This is the crack running between our two hearts that turned into a valley and engulfed us. It's my acceptance of all I couldn't bridge.

This is me knowing that we don't get a do-over—not on the last night I spent asleep beside you, the last time I told you I loved you, or the first moment I felt us start to drift apart. I know we don't always get second chances. I know I do not get to go back in time and kiss you slower, love you stronger, and linger five extra minutes in bed every morning that I woke up beside you. This is me knowing that I can't rewind history and ask you what was wrong each evening that you came home with a puzzle in your eyes but no answer on your lips. This is me knowing we don't get to go back.

This is my acceptance that I'm going to miss you. That there are going to be nights when I curl up in bed with a novel and a warm mug of tea, and your absence on the left side of the bed is a chasm that swells and envelopes me. That for a long time, I am going to see you everywhere—in second-floor windows, in the faces of strangers, in the photos and memories that tear at my heartstrings for months after you're gone. This is the realization that missing you will become a second heartbeat in my body, strong and thrumming inside every place where you lingered and then left. These are my weakened vital signs, beating out of sync with yours for a while.

This is my knowing life goes on. Knowing that someday, I will not think of love as a feeling exclusive to you and I, as crazy as that seems to me right now. That eventually, I'll meet someone new—someone who loves the foods you hate, laughs at things you don't find funny, and appreciates the parts of me that you once left undiscovered. That some days, in the early morning hours, I'm going to wake up beside them and forget—just for an instant—that it is not your body tangled in mine. This is me knowing that those moments will defeat me—that I'm going to need to practice standing at the edge of your abyss without falling in completely. This is my hope: the discrepancy shrivels with time.

This is my conceptualization: That someday, I'm going to have a wedding, and that you will not be there. That the ring that gets slipped on my finger will be picked out by somebody else and that the people sitting in the front row with eyes brimming and hearts bursting will not be your family members. This is my acceptance of the finite absurdity of knowing that I will someday promise my life to someone who is not you and that I may even be happy to do so. That one day, I'll see changes and beginnings in a way I never saw them with you.

This is me knowing that we're going to grow old. That your life is going to be huge and important and chock-full of love, but that it's all going to transpire without me. I will not be there to toast your 50th birthday, cheer for your timely promotion, or crawl in bed beside you on the nights when the world's weight is too heavy to bear. That your losses and gains will not be lined up with mine. That someday, when you hold your firstborn child in your arms, it won't be me who placed her there.

This is me knowing that I have to let you go. That no matter how much I love you, how hard we work at this, or how badly we both want each other to be happy, we are never going to be the right partners for each other. This is my acceptance that the best things are never straightforward and that I want you to take whatever crooked, twisted path you need to take if it will lead you towards your dreams. This is me knowing that I have to do what's right. That sometimes, the best thing you can do for someone you love is to let them go—to do more, feel more, and be more than the person they could ever have become by your side.

So this is me unclasping my fingers.

This is my parting, my reluctance, my heartache, and my final gift to you.

This is me letting you go.

Heidi Priebe is the author of *The First New Universe,*
The Comprehensive ENFP Survival Guide, and
The Comprehensive INFP Survival Guide.

instagram.com/heidipriebe
youtube.com/@heidipriebe1

Other THOUGHT CATALOG titles
published by AMARYLLIS in India

THE PIVOT YEAR

THE MOUNTAIN IS YOU

WHEN YOU'RE READY THIS IS HOW YOU HEAL

101 ESSAYS THAT WILL CHANGE THE WAY YOU THINK

CEREMONY

THIS WAS MEANT TO FIND YOU:
WHEN YOU NEEDED IT MOST

SALT WATER

EVERYTHING YOU'LL EVER NEED
YOU CAN FIND WITHIN YOURSELF

THE HUMAN ELEMENT

THE STRENGTH IN OUR SCARS

THE TRUTH ABOUT EVERYTHING

ALL THE WORDS I SHOULD HAVE SAID

BEAUTY IN THE STILLNESS

YOU'RE OVERTHINKING IT